GOLD MEDAL GUIDE

Golden tips for keeping your first
RABBIT

AMANDA O'NEILL

Interpet Publishing

Editor: Philip de Ste. Croix
Designer: Phil Clucas MSIAD
Studio photography:
Neil Sutherland
Production management:
Consortium, Poslingford, Suffolk

Print production:
SNP Leefung Printers Ltd.
Printed and bound
in the Far East

Published by Interpet Publishing,
Vincent Lane, Dorking,
Surrey RH4 3YX, England

© 2004 Interpet Publishing Ltd.
This reprint 2007

ISBN 978-1-84286-092-2

The Author Amanda O'Neill was born in Sussex in 1951 and educated at the University of Exeter, where she read medieval literature. She has never lived without a variety of pets, ranging from rabbits and gerbils to giant snails and hissing cockroaches. Currently she lives in the Midlands with her husband and son, along with five dogs, a cat, Roborowski hamsters and a collection of coldwater fish.

The recommendations in this book are given without any guarantees on the part of the author and publisher. If in doubt, seek the advice of a vet or pet-care specialist.

Contents

INTRODUCTION

Right: Don't try carrying your rabbit around like this until he trusts you enough not to make a flying leap!

1 Rabbits make great pets – if you're prepared to be a great owner

Rabbits are cheap and easy to house and care for, and, given plenty of time and attention, they are responsive, affectionate and entertaining animals. Without this input from you, however, your rabbit will make a very unrewarding pet. Too often, rabbits are kept in solitary confinement in tiny hutches with nothing to do, and then their owners complain that they are boring. So, before you adopt a rabbit, be sure that you want to spend time with him every day.

2 Tame rabbits have a long history

The species has been kept in domestication since at least Roman times. Their wild ancestors originated in the Mediterranean region, but have since been introduced by man across Europe, into the British Isles, Australia, New Zealand, the USA and elsewhere. For centuries, domestic rabbits were kept simply for meat and fur. Originally they were housed in large enclosures called warrens, but as more people took up town life, they started keeping rabbits in hutches to supply them with meat. The idea of keeping them as pets is as recent as the nineteenth century.

Hay rack

Feeding bowls

Water bottle

SHOPPING LIST
Before you bring your rabbit home, you will need a hutch, food bowl, water bottle, food, bedding, and some form of exercise area. The rabbit should be the last item on your shopping list.

A LONG LIFESPAN
Unlike mice and hamsters, many rabbits run the risk of outliving their young owners' interest. So before you buy a rabbit, be aware that it is likely to be with you for some eight to ten years.

RABBITS AND CHILDREN
Rabbits are only suitable pets for older children, and parental supervision is needed. A small child is not strong enough to hold a rabbit securely. The rabbit may be hurt, and – just as importantly – so may the child.

Rabbits are not toys

3

They may look cuddly, but they have all the instincts of their wild ancestors. Wild rabbits are prey animals, hunted by many other species. They are easily alarmed and are programmed to respond to a scare by flight, freezing or lashing out, depending on the circumstances. They are also ground-dwellers who hate being held above ground-level – something that would only happen in the wild when a rabbit is captured by a predator. Your pet has to learn to trust you before he can relax in the human environment and enjoy being handled.

GOLD MEDAL
TIPS

VARIETIES

4

Rabbits come in many colours, sizes, coats and temperaments

From small, brown wild rabbits, man has developed more than 50 breeds in many colours and in sizes varying from giants bigger than a cat to miniatures that fit in your hand. Fur types include Rexes, with short plush coats, Satins, with smooth, very shiny coats, and longhairs from fluffy Cashmere Lops to profusely coated Angoras – even the recently developed Lionhead, with a short body coat and a long mane around the neck.

5

For a laid-back character, consider the giant breeds

The largest, such as Flemish Giants and French Lops, are about three times the size of a wild rabbit, weighing around 11.5kg (25lb). Generally they have a calmer temperament than the small and miniature breeds, and make gentle pets. On the debit side, they need larger accommodation, and are too big for most children to handle comfortably. They also have a shorter lifespan, maybe as little as four to five years.

Cute, but not so cuddly

Mini-rabbits, such as Polish and Netherland Dwarfs (right), are enchantingly pretty. They tend to be more nervous and highly-strung than their larger relations, and are more likely to nip, so they are not recommended as children's pets. However, many individuals respond to gentle handling and become confident, cocky little characters who are great fun to have around. They are also among the longer-lived breeds, averaging ten to 12 years.

Above: Chocolate Havana

Above: English Spot

Above: Ermine Rex

Above: This white Angora is not the best choice for a novice..

Longhairs are only for the dedicated

Angoras were developed for their wool, not as a fur breed. Their massive coats are regularly shorn like a sheep's to provide a very soft, fine wool for spinning – about 1kg (2.2lb) per rabbit per year. Such a coat is far too much for a rabbit to look after itself, and requires daily grooming by the owner to prevent it from matting into solid lumps. If you don't find this daily task enjoyable, don't take on an Angora!

CHOOSING A RABBIT

Moving home is stressful for a rabbit

Where possible, buy your rabbit direct from the breeder – pet-shop rabbits have already moved home once and have been exposed to extra stress, as well as to disease. Stress makes an animal vulnerable to illness and can even kill, and in any case you do not want a pet which is a bundle of nerves. The tamer the rabbit, the more calmly it will take a change of circumstances, so if the breeder's stock is wild and nervous, go elsewhere.

Above: Baby rabbits under six weeks old are far from ready to leave home.

Clean ears

Bright eyes

Clea nos

Level te

Dewlap ('double chin') acceptab on adult large-breed rabbits

Well-rounded rump

Well-covered body, not fat and flabby or thin with visible ribs

Clean tail

Well-furred hocks

Not fat

Short nails

Start with a healthy animal

When buying a rabbit, look for an animal which is alert with bright, clear eyes and soft shiny fur. Avoid any animal which has runny eyes, a runny nose, bald patches or a dirty bottom – or whose cage-mates display these signs. The ideal age is about six weeks, and by then a young rabbit should be accustomed to handling. Youngsters which have never been handled before sale will take a great deal of work to make them into happy pets.

Male or female?

Individuals vary, and either sex can make a good pet. However, if in doubt, a buck (male) is usually the better choice. Does (females) can often become territorial and aggressive when they are sexually mature, whereas bucks tend to have a more even temperament and are usually more playful. Bucks are more likely to spray urine as a territorial marker, and some may develop the habit of mounting an owner's arm or leg.

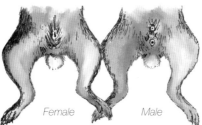

Female   Male

One rabbit or two?

Rabbits need company, but housing two rabbits together is not easy. Two males will fight to the death. A male and female will breed – non-stop. Two females, especially litter sisters, may live together, but often one will bully the other when they reach maturity. The only really safe combination is two neutered rabbits. Neutering just one won't help – the other, with hormones intact, is likely to attack its companion. One rabbit, given enough human company, is the easiest solution.

SETTLING IN

When you bring your rabbit home, put him in his cage and leave him alone to adjust. For the first couple of days, just feed and water him, but don't handle him – unless he is already very tame. Let him make friends with you at his own pace.

GUINEA PIGS

Keeping a guinea pig as a companion for your rabbit is not recommended. Rabbits are tougher and more territorial than guinea pigs and tend to bully them. If you decide to try it, introduce the animals when they are both young and keep a close eye on their relationship throughout their lives.

RESCUE A RABBIT

Consider adopting a rabbit from an animal charity. There are thousands of unwanted rabbits in need of a home. By recycling an abandoned pet, you save its life – with the further advantage that the charity will help you to choose your pet.

GOLD MEDAL
TIPS

HOUSING

The bigger the hutch, the better

Rabbits are active creatures and need room to move. The biggest hutch you can fit in will be the best. At the very least, it must be tall enough for your rabbit to sit up and long enough for him to stretch out in comfort and move about a bit. Rabbits vary greatly in size, but on average 120cm (48in) is a good length. Many commercially produced hutches are far too small and amount to prison cells rather than homes. Ideally, the hutch should have one end partitioned off to provide secluded sleeping quarters.

Above: A good quality of wire mesh protects your rabbit.

WATCH THE WIRE

Wire mesh on cage-fronts needs to be small-gauge to keep out mice, which can pop through larger gaps in search of food and so spread disease. It also needs to be strong and securely attached to keep out predators. To any passing dog, cat or fox, your pet is a potential dinner.

Beware of draughts and damp

Never place a hutch directly on the ground, but raise it on legs so that air circulates beneath, protecting both hutch and occupant from damp. Outdoor hutches need weatherproofing, using non-toxic wood preservatives, and a sloping roof to let rain to drain off. The hutch should be in a sheltered position, away from draughts. If rain is likely to drive directly in through the front, you will need a protective canopy for wet weather. Heat is equally dangerous, so make sure the hutch is not in direct sunlight during the day to protect your pet from the risk of heat-stroke.

FLAWED FLOORS

Commercial rabbit breeders favour wire-mesh floors to reduce work in cleaning out. However, these are undesirable for pet rabbits. Wire floors are less comfortable for your pet to walk on, claws may catch in them, and thinner-furred breeds are likely to develop sore feet from this surface.

NEEDS

Below: A practical cage for indoor use.

House rabbits

14

Rabbits make good indoor pets and can be house-trained to use a litter tray. You will still need a hutch or cage as a base to which your rabbit can retire when he wants privacy, or where you can shut him in when necessary. Young rabbits can be as destructive as kittens or puppies and need supervision. Rooms to which the rabbit has access need to be vetted for safety. All rabbits chew, so danger zones such as electrical wires and sockets must be rabbit-proofed.

THE ESSENTIAL EQUIPMENT

15

Right: A sturdy pottery bowl is unlikely to tip over easily.

Bottles are best

A water bottle clipped to the front of the hutch is better than a water bowl. It avoids risks of spillage or fouling of the water, and enables you to see at a glance whether your rabbit is drinking or not. Do remember to change the water daily, and take the opportunity to check that the ball valve is working. Hold the bottle nozzle downwards and squeeze it gently: if no water squirts out, the valve may be clogged or otherwise damaged. Some rabbits tend to chew the metal nozzle, and can crush it so that no water gets through.

16

The perfect food bowl

Food bowls should be heavy enough not to tip over easily. Metal bowls are often too lightweight, while plastic is not only light but dangerous, as rabbits will chew it and may cut themselves or even swallow pieces, causing stomach blockages. You can buy plastic bowls with hooks which clip on to the cage front, but many rabbits will enjoy unhooking these and spilling the contents. Pottery bowls have the advantage of being heavy and easy to clean.

17

Bedding material

The hutch floor should be covered with safe and absorbent bedding materials, such as sawdust, straw, wood shavings, peat or shredded paper. Sawdust and shavings must be clean – if you obtain these from a wood mill, make sure they contain no chemical preservatives. Layers of newspaper spread over the cage floor before strewing the bedding on top provide extra absorbency. It's simple to roll up the paper with the used bedding inside. Inside the sleeping quarters, add plenty of hay for a soft bed and bedtime nibbles.

GOLD MEDAL TIPS

RACK NOT RUIN
A hay rack which clips on to the wall of the hutch is useful to prevent hay (other than that in the sleeping quarters) from being trampled and soiled. It allows the rabbit to pull down what it wants to eat at the time, keeping the rest safe for later.

A CHEAP BEDROOM
If your rabbit's hutch doesn't have separate sleeping quarters, use a cardboard box placed at one end. This provides the darkness and privacy a rabbit prefers for its bedroom. It will soon become soggy and chewed, but you can simply replace it every week.

TOILET TRAINING
A cat-litter tray can make cleaning out easier. Most rabbits select one corner of the hutch for soiling, so try a cat-litter tray filled with sawdust in the toilet corner. Add a little soiled bedding to remind the rabbit what this corner is for.

FOOD AND

There are two basic rabbit diets

You can feed hay and vegetables – plenty of hay, daily greens and a small amount of cereal or commercial rabbit mix. Greens must be clean and fresh – wash bought vegetables, don't pick grass from roadside verges, and avoid lawn clippings. Alternatively you can feed dry food – proprietary rabbit mixes or pellets, which form a complete diet, plus hay. Keep all dry food in mouse-proof containers to avoid contamination. Either diet is acceptable, but stick to one – don't chop and change.

Hay forms the basis of a healthy diet

Hay goes a long way towards meeting a rabbit's nutritional needs, and its tough fibres maintain healthy gut movement and sound teeth. Nibbling hay also helps to reduce boredom and consequent behavioural problems. Good quality hay is essential. Avoid any that is dusty or musty-smelling, and always store hay where air can circulate – not in sealed plastic bags. Try different kinds – meadow hay, seed hay, kiln-dried grass – and see what your rabbit prefers. If in doubt, meadow hay is always a safe choice.

FEEDING

Feed on a regular timetable

Feed your rabbit twice daily, morning and night. This means your pet has two visits to look forward to, and you can make regular checks on his well-being. The amount of food a rabbit requires will depend on his age and size. If the hutch is stripped bare of food when you arrive, increase the portions. If there is quite a lot food left, reduce them. Any greens left over should be thrown away, as stale greens can cause digestive upsets.

Left: Your rabbit will thrive on a diet of hay and dry food, if you do not choose to feed greens.

Fresh water must be available at all times

Rabbits which eat a lot of greens may not drink much, as they obtain most of their liquid intake from their food. Rabbits on a dry food mix may drink a great deal more. Even if you never see your rabbit drinking, make sure water is always available and changed daily. In winter, water may freeze, so only half-fill the bottle so that it does not crack, and allow extra time to thaw out the ice and replace with fresh water.

GOLD MEDAL TIPS

DON'T CHANGE

Find out what your rabbit has been fed on before you buy it and stick to that initially. Sudden change, especially for baby rabbits, can be fatal. Never change diet suddenly. Take at least a week to switch between different brands of dry food or to introduce greens into diet.

CHEWING THE CUD

Don't be alarmed if your rabbit eats its droppings. Raw vegetables take a lot of digesting, so, like cows chewing the cud, rabbits eat their food twice! They produce soft droppings which they then eat to get the full value out of their food (as well as hard droppings which are waste).

DANGEROUS PLANTS

Beware – a number of common garden plants are toxic and may cause death if a rabbit eats them. Examples of plants that pose a health threat are anemones, elder, figwort, foxgloves, poppies, nightshade, wild clematis and many bulbs.

TREATS AND TI

Melon *Carrot cake*

22

Healthy snacks are best

Hand-feeding special titbits is a great way to increase your rabbit's confidence in you. On the other hand, too many titbits are as bad for rabbits as for any other species. The occasional carbohydrate treat such as a piece of biscuit or cake or a commercial

Banana

Above: If your rabbit is not used to greens, remove all but a few leaves from branches.

treat like yogurt drops or cereal sticks is fine, but it is bes to stick to healthy snacks like apple cores, carrot chunks broccoli florets, or turnip peelings. Bits of wholemeal brea dried in the oven until hard make good occasional nibble and help to maintain dental health.

23

Fieldberry treats

Left: A range of fruit and vegetable titbits make meals fun and supplement your pet's diet. You will soon learn which are his favourites.

Apple

ar

Rabbits need something to chew

Their teeth grow constantly (up to 13cm/5in a year!) and a rabbit with nothing to chew will soon suffer from overgrown teeth. You can buy commercially made chew blocks, but one of the best answers to the rabbit's dental demands is a length of branch wedged in his cage. Not all trees are suitable, but you cannot go wrong with wood from any fruit tree (apple, pear, plum, etc.). If your rabbit is used to eating greens, leave the leaves on the branch for an extra treat, but remove any fruit, especially if it is unripe.

Left: When collecting a branch for your rabbit, be careful to avoid any fruit tree which has been sprayed with pesticides.

Above: Healthy treats are a great way to win your pet's trust.

24

Fresh fruit should be given in moderation

Too much fruit will cause diarrhoea, which can be fatal. Dwarf rabbits in particular tend to have delicate digestions, and may be safer on a fruit-free regime. But a small daily portion is an enjoyable and healthy treat for most rabbits. s a rough guide, allow one tablespoon of fruit per 2kg (4.5lb) bodyweight (half the nount if using dried fruit). Apple, pineapple, banana, melon, peach, pear, strawberry nd raspberry are all suitable. Always wash fruit before feeding it to your rabbit to move any traces of chemicals or preservatives.

Rabbits need daily exercise

Rabbits need daily exercise, ideally in a secure run which can be moved around the garden. Giving your pet free run of the garden is advisable only if the garden is completely escape-proof and you are sure not a single plant is poisonous to rabbits. Even then, you should supervise him in case a hungry cat, stray dog or fox jumps over the fence. Obviously, on some days the weather will not permit outdoor exercise, and it is useful to rabbit-proof a room in the house so that on those days your rabbit can enjoy running around the house instead.

PLAY AND EXERCISE

26

Sunstroke can kill – and so can a chill

Below: Rabbits appreciate cosy corners and hidey-holes to explore.

When leaving your rabbit in his run, make sure he has shelter from direct sunlight. Remember that an area which is shaded in the morning may be fully exposed to the sun by afternoon. On hot days, draping a cloth over the run is a sensible safety measure. Rabbits also need protection from rain. A rabbit's fur is easily soaked, and a wet rabbit is a chilled rabbit. If your rabbit gets wet, gently towel-dry his fur as much as possible and then keep him indoors in a box full of hay until he has dried out.

GOLD MEDAL TIPS

A healthy rabbit enjoys playtime

In general, rabbits are playful creatures – specially bucks. If your rabbit just sits around looking morose, something is wrong! Racing around, jumping and leaping are natural ways for a healthy rabbit to burn off surplus energy – and he needs space to do this. You can make play-time more interesting by putting boxes or drainpipe tunnels in your pet's run for him to explore and jump on and off. Some rabbits enjoy nosing a ball around the garden. Two rabbits will play chase games, but only a very confident rabbit enjoys playing chase with humans – it's too much like being hunted.

Above: Make sure that a harness fits well, neither too tight for comfort nor too loose for safety.

Left: Rabbits feel safer if some shelter is available to them.

HARNESSES
Lightweight nylon rabbit harnesses can be useful as a safety restraint for pottering around the garden. Always let your pet lead you: don't pull him along. Don't try to take your pet for walks in the park like a dog – he will not enjoy it.

CATS AND DOGS
Cats and dogs are a rabbit's natural enemies, but if they are brought up together and supervised they can become friends who will enjoy playing together. However, play time should always be monitored.

HEALTHY SUNSHINE
Outdoor exercise is important, as exposure to sunlight allows rabbits to manufacture Vitamin D, which helps the body to use dietary calcium. Rabbits shut in hutches or kept indoors are denied this opportunity.

GROOMING

28

Rabbits take good care of their coats – but you can help

Fur needs daily care, and rabbits use teeth and claws as combs to keep their coats in good condition. However, you can help with a weekly gentle comb-through with a cat comb to remove any surplus dead hair. Grooming also helps to develop your relationship with your pet and gives you a chance to make a regular check on skin health, looking out for fleas, wounds and any other problems. Long-haired breeds, of course, need daily grooming, using a soft brush.

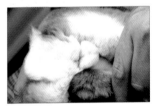

Above: A daily hygiene check only takes a moment.

29

Moulting rabbits need extra assistance

Wild rabbits moult twice a year, but domestic rabbits vary – some moult continuously, especially if they live indoors in centrally heated houses. A moult can be very heavy – you may find the hutch full of shed fur. There is a risk that a moulting rabbit may swallow large amounts of dead hair while grooming, which can clog the gut. Daily grooming during the moult reduces the risk, and helps the rabbit to keep on top of coat care.

OR HEALTH

icker brush

Soft brush

Keep an eye on claws

Overgrown claws can
eventually curve round to grow into the flesh. Make
a claw check part of your regular routine. If the
claws need clipping, ask your vet to show you the
correct technique. If you cut too short, you will cause
pain and bleeding. With white claws, it is easy to see
the pink 'quick' and cut below, but dark claws require
extra care. If you make a mistake, press the injured
claw into a damp bar of soap to stop the bleeding.

Nail clippers

Hygiene wipes

Below: Be gentle when brushing your pet.

Above: Overgrown claws make walking and grooming difficult for your rabbit.

Check the tail area for any soiling.

Rabbits' teeth grow throughout their lives

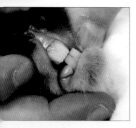

Normally, chewing keeps them down
to the right length. But if a rabbit lacks chewing opportunities,
has a poor diet, or has inherited dental problems, teeth can
grow too long, making eating difficult. Make a dental check part
of your weekly routine. Warning signs include eating problems
and dribbling. Once a rabbit's teeth have gone wrong, they will
need regular attention from the vet.

Daily housekeeping

A little light housekeeping every day keeps the hutch pleasant. Each day, remove wet bedding and clear heavily soiled areas (usually the favoured toilet corner), replacing with clean dry sawdust or whichever bedding you favour. Make sure ther is enough hay in the bedroom for comfort. Catering and washing-up should also be don daily. Remove any uneaten food from the bowl and wash and dry the bowl before refilling Wash and refill the wate bottle, checking fc leaks and blockages

HUTCH HYGIENE

Below: Most rabbits can be persuaded to use a litter tray filled with sawdust.

Don't expect your rabbit to appreciate your efforts!

Rabbits are territorial, and as far as they are concerned you are simply barging into their home and rearranging the furniture. To a rabbit, his droppings and urine are smell markers that affirm his identity and his home ownership. He may express his objections by barging around and getting in your way, or he may even nip. Be patient, and he will grow used to the routine. If he nips, wear gloves.

Weekly routine

Once a week, the hutch should be cleaned thoroughly. Remove everything and brush it out thoroughly before giving it a good scrub. In summer, scrub with hot soapy water, paying special attention to the corners, rinse well and allow the hutch to dry out thoroughly before replacing bedding materials. In winter, a wet cage may never dry, so substitute a light wipe-over with mild disinfectant.

Safety measures

When cleaning out, check the hutch for early signs of damage and danger areas. Perhaps the rabbit has started chewing at the timber, when you may need to do some repair work before there is a large hole – and ensure that he has something more suitable to chew in future. Urine may have soaked through the bedding in a corner, making the wood soggy and likely to rot, and this corner will need extra attention. Wire mesh can sometimes work loose, leaving dangerous sharp edges which could cause injury. All such problems are best picked up early, before any real harm ensues.

Rabbits have great long-distance eyesight

36

Their near-distance vision isn't so good. A human hand appearing in front of a rabbit's face can be very startling to him. Until your rabbit is used to you, keep your hands above his head and away from his nose. If your rabbit nips when hand-fed, this again may be due to poor eyesight and you can solve the problem by using larger treats, such as a long grass-stem, until the rabbit learns what is food and what are fingers.

UNDERSTANDING YOUR RABBIT

37

Rabbits don't use much vocal language

Cats and dogs communicate with meows or barks and other sounds. Rabbits don't. They have a restricted range of vocal sounds, limited to sniffs (curious, conversational or annoyed), grunts (angry, and a warning to back off or be bitten), tooth-grinding (usually a sign of contentment) and screams (only in extreme pain or terror). They communicate more with body language, and you will soon learn to recognize their emotions.

38

The sense of smell is important to rabbits

Rabbits have a much better sense of smell than humans. Different scents make them feel secure or insecure. To a rabbit, spreading his own smell around his territory (which he does with urine and droppings, and also using scent glands under his chin) makes the place feel like home. Alien scents, such as that of a passing strange dog, are alarming to him. You will need to allow time for a new pet to grow accustomed to your smell.

Above: Rabbits rely on the sense of smell to find food, as well as to detect danger.

Sounding the alarm

39

Wild rabbits warn each other of impending danger by stamping loudly on the ground. Tame rabbits react to anything they perceive as danger in the same way. Stamping on a hutch floor can make a surprisingly loud noise, and a nervous rabbit can make you unpopular with the neighbours! Such pets should be moved to a quieter location for their own peace of mind as well as noise prevention. Some rabbits will also use the stamping signal to summon their owners.

TOOTHY TALK
Rabbits may nip out of fear or aggression. But your pet may also use nipping to communicate with you. A light nip may be intended to tell you that he has had enough attention and wants to be put down, or that he wants a titbit or wishes to investigate something.

DIFFERENT PERSONALITIES
Rabbits are individuals. Some are naturally nervous, some naturally bold. Some are more playful than others. If you want a friendly rabbit, your best bet is to choose a youngster from notably friendly parents, or alternatively to adopt an adult whose personality is already known.

Above: Make friends with your rabbit at ground level to win his confidence.

GROUND RULES
To a rabbit, humans are huge. It's easier to make friends if you get down to his level. Crouching or even lying flat on the ground makes you smaller and more approachable. Until your rabbit is confident with you, don't force yourself upon him, but let him make the advances.

GOLD MEDAL TIPS

KEEP OFF THE EARS

Never, ever pick a rabbit up by his ears. Although you may hear old-fashioned breeders talk about this method, it is painful for the rabbit and can damage muscles and ear membranes. You wouldn't treat any other pet in this way, so don't do it to a defenceless rabbit!

TRANSPORT OF DELIGHT

If you are taking your rabbit out, to the vet or anywhere else, never carry him in your arms, no matter how tame he is. There is always the chance, however small, that something may startle him and make him break free. Always transport him inside a safe carrier.

SPECIAL TREATMENT

Be prepared for female rabbits to change character dramatically when they have babies in the nest. Your sweet, friendly doe may become quite fierce and attack your hands when you go near. You will have to make allowances at such times – and wear gloves when tending her until the babies are weaned.

HANDLING YOUR RABBIT

Being picked up is a scary experience

Until your rabbit is used to being handled, he will fight – and rabbits are surprisingly strong. Make him feel as secure as possible. Put one hand round his chest behind the forelegs, and as you lift him, support his rump with the other hand. Bring him against your body, keeping him supported. If he is nervous, keep his back against you and his legs facing outwards, to avoid being kicked. When he is more confident, you can hold him sideways on for comfort, and eventually he will snuggle down in your arms and enjoy the experience.

Beware of the claws!

Rabbits who are unused to handling wriggle and kick out. Their hind legs pack a powerful punch, and the strong claws can slash your arm quite painfully. The forelegs are weaker, but still have sharp claws which can leave you covered in scratches. Your rabbit has no intention of hurting you – he just wants to escape – but that is small comfort. So take a few precautions. While you and your rabbit are learning to trust each other, take care to keep his legs aimed away from you, and never pick up your pet when you have bare arms.

Right: Powerful hind legs provide propulsion for running and for defensive kicking. The rear paws are much larger, and stronger, than the rather dainty front paws.

Left: Held like this, the rabbit is supported below and on both sides so that he is safe and secure. Never hold even the tamest rabbit in a position where he might feel vulnerable, or one of you may end up being hurt.

Below: Offering a titbit is a good way to demonstrate that your intentions are friendly – though a timid rabbit may take some time to accept this fact.

42 Occasionally you will meet an aggressive rabbit

A really bad-tempered rabbit can be quite scary, and can do you considerable damage with his teeth and claws. Some are aggressive through fear, often because they have been mishandled in the past.

Such rabbits can be re-educated to become affectionate and rewarding pets, but it takes a lot of time and patience. Daily sessions of gentle talking and very gentle handling can eventually win a rabbit round – but first kit yourself out with protective clothing, including rabbit-proof gloves, to avoid injury. Another cause of aggression is hormonal. Some females can be very fierce when in season, in which case spaying is recommended. Mothers with young may also be aggressive until the babies are successfully weaned.

HEALTHCARE AND AILMENTS

43

Handling your pet daily is the best health check

You can spot any symptoms before matters become serious. A sick rabbit is usually lethargic and loses its appetite. He will stay hunched at the back of his hutch instead of coming to greet you. A runny nose and noisy breathing warn of respiratory infection, which will need antibiotics. A bloated abdomen means a blocked gut, which may be caused by a change in diet, too many greens, or fur balls blocking the stomach. Whatever the cause it requires immediate veterinary care.

44

Droppings are a guide to your rabbit's health

Healthy droppings are neat, hard balls. Rabbits also regularly produce soft droppings which are eaten (see page 15), so don't worry if you see a few of these. However, a large amount of soft droppings means diarrhoea ('scours'). In mild cases, withdrawing all greens and serving only dry food will cure the problem – severe cases need veterinary treatment. The opposite condition, when droppings are notably fewer and drier than usual, may indicate a blocked gut, when a trip to the vet is certainly needed.

45 Vaccinate against viruses

Left: Vitamin drops may be a useful supplement to the diet for indoor rabbits.

Two serious viral diseases which can affect rabbits are myxomatosis and viral haemmorhagic disease. Both are usually fatal. Myxomatosis is spread by biting insects, and it is thought that VHD may spread in the same way, so rabbits don't have to be exposed to other rabbits to be vulnerable. Your rabbit can be protected against these viruses by vaccination, which is strongly recommended. Ask your local vet for advice on vaccinations and also on annual boosters to keep the protection up to date.

46 Beware of the flea!

You may not spot these tiny parasites on your rabbit, but watch out for gritty black particles in his fur – telltale flea droppings. Fleas spread disease, so tackle them straightaway, using a flea spray guaranteed safe for rabbits. Treat the hutch, too, to kill flea eggs. Rabbits are also vulnerable to fur mites, which attack the skin (look for scabby patches), and ear mites inside the ears (look for itching and a smelly, dark discharge).

GOLD MEDAL
TIPS

RING CHECK
If your rabbit arrives with a metal ring (used for show rabbits) on one hind leg, do check this regularly throughout his life. It should be loose enough to turn easily around the leg. Occasionally the ring becomes too tight with time, and needs to be cut off before it causes injury to the leg.

ON THE SCALES
A weekly weigh-in is a handy method of monitoring your pet's health. The scales may show any change of weight before you would normally notice it. Any sudden weight change needs investigation. You will need to accustom your rabbit to the scales before he feels confident enough to sit still.

HEATSTROKE
Rabbits are very vulnerable to heat. Heatstroke victims should be wrapped in a thick towel which has been soaked in cold water and wrung out. Prevention is better than cure, so don't leave a rabbit unprotected in full sun, or shut in a badly ventilated hutch on a hot day.

BREEDING ADVICE

Think before you breed!

Before you go ahead, the three rules are: know why you have chosen to breed this litter, make sure you breed only from healthy, well-handled animals, and know what you will do with the babies. Please, don't breed from your rabbit unless you have a good reason to do so. There are already far more rabbits being bred than there are good homes for them, so don't add to the numbers of unwanted pets.

Good breeding practice

Always take the doe to the buck's hutch for mating, never the other way round, and return her to her own hutch afterwards. Pregnancy lasts about 30 days, during which period the doe should be handled as little as possible, especially in the later days. Gradually double her rations, and about 25 days after mating provide her with a nest box and extra bedding. When she is due to give birth, she will start plucking her fur to line the nest.

49 Newborn rabbits are blind and helpless

When the birth is completed, check for any dead babies which need to be removed, but otherwise try to disturb the new mother as little as possible during the early days. Although you may be impatient to view the new arrivals, this may agitate the doe to the point where she kills her babies. Increase her rations to about three times the normal amount while she is suckling, and make sure she always has clean water available.

Below: Baby rabbits (kittens) at about three weeks old.

50 Baby rabbits grow surprisingly fast

Their eyes open on about the tenth day, and soon afterwards they will leave the nest and start exploring. At this stage, increase the food supply again as they start nibbling solid food. At six to eight weeks, the young rabbits should be weaned. Remove the mother, and a few days later divide the babies into single-sex groups. They are now ready to leave home.

HOW MANY BABIES?
The average litter size is five, but it varies according to the breed. In general, big rabbits have big litters, and tiny breeds have tiny litters. A first-time mother often has a smaller litter than usual, and may lose her first babies through inexperience – she will usually fare better next time.

NESTBOXES
A nestbox should be about 30-45cm (12-18in) long and 20-30cm (8-12in) wide, depending on the size of the doe. It only needs to be about 5cm (2in) deep. Plywood is ideal, but you can use a cardboard carton cut down to size. Fill it with absorbent shavings and then soft hay.

Above: A tame, friendly mother makes for tame babies.

FALSE PREGNANCY
Sometimes a doe, mated or not, will appear to be pregnant and will even prepare a nest, but no babies will appear. This is termed a 'false pregnancy'. Does which are never used for breeding may have frequent false pregnancies, and such females will be happier spayed.

Further Information

Recommended Books

Alderton, David, *A Petlove Guide to Rabbits and Guinea Pigs* (Interpet Publishing, 1986)

Bartlett, Patricia, *Training Your Pet Rabbit* (Barron's, 2002)

Brown, Meg, and Richardson, Virginia, *Rabbitlopedia, A Complete Guide to Rabbit Care* (Ringpress Books, 2000)

Dykes, Linda, and Flack, Helen, *Living With A Houserabbit* (Interpet Publishing, 2003)

Gendron, Karen, *The Rabbit Handbook* (Barron's, 2000)

Harriman, Marinell, *The House Rabbit Handbook* (Drollery Press, 1995)

Hearne, Tina, *Care For Your Rabbit* (RSPCA Guide; Collins 1990)

Leewood, Hazel, *Pet Owner's Guide to the Dwarf Rabbit* (Ringpress Books, 1999)

Mays, Marianne, *Pet Owner's Guide to the Rabbit* (Ringpress Books, 1995)

McBride, Anne, *Why Does My Rabbit....?* (Souvenir Press, 2000)

Page, Gill, *Getting To Know Your Rabbit* (Interpet Publishing , 2000)

Siino, Betsy Sikora, *The Essential Rabbit* (Howell Book House, 1998)

Wegler, Monica, *Rabbits – A Complete Pet Owner's Manual* (Barron's, 1999)

Clubs

American Rabbit Breeders' Association, PO Box 426, Bloomington, IL 61702, USA

British Rabbit Council, Purefoy House, 7 Kirkgate, Newark, Nottinghamshire, NG24 1AD, UK

The Rabbit Charity, PO Box 23698, London, N8 0WS, UK

Recommended Websites

http://www.allaboutpets.org.uk/spintro.html

http://www.rabbit.org/chapters/san-diego

http://www.rabbitwelfarefund.co.uk

Acknowledgements

The author and publisher would like to offer sincere thanks to Jackie Wilson of Rolf C. Hagen (UK) Ltd who generously supplied equipment for photography in this book. Thanks also go to models Florence Elphick and Michael Newman, to Holmbush Farm World, Faygate who provided rabbits for photography, to Nottcutts Garden Centre, Cranleigh for the loan of a hutch, and to Peter Dean at Interpet Ltd for his help with photographic props.

Picture Credits

The majority of the photographs reproduced were taken by Neil Sutherland specifically for this book. All photographs included in the book are the copyright of Interpet Publishing.